WE ARE Mighty

12 Ordinary Americans Who Did the Next Needed Thing

written by

Sharon McMahon

illustrated by

Susanna Chapman

Alfred A. Knopf
New York

For my children, and for yours

—S.M.

For the ordinary, brave voice in you and in me

—S.C.

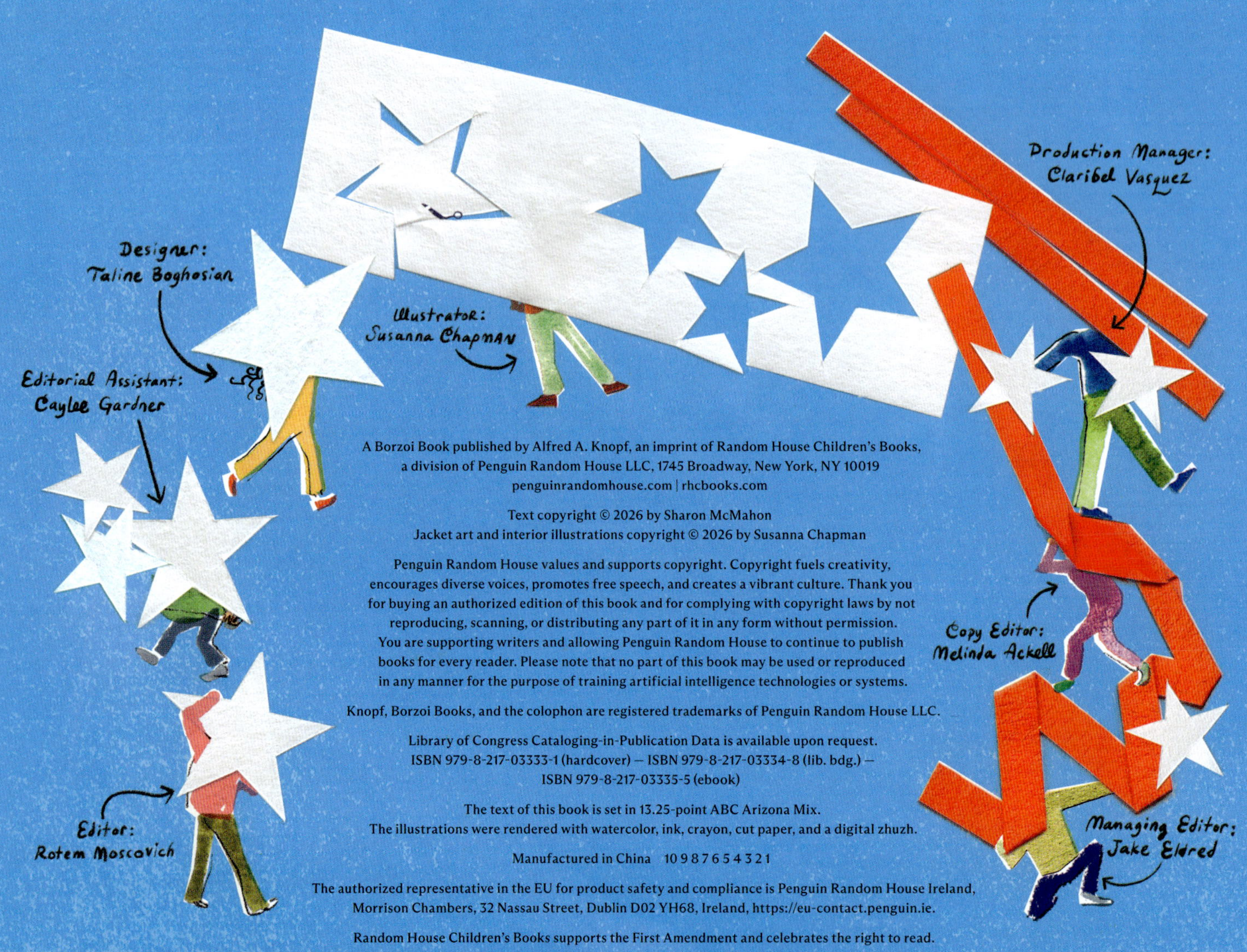

A Borzoi Book published by Alfred A. Knopf, an imprint of Random House Children's Books, a division of Penguin Random House LLC, 1745 Broadway, New York, NY 10019
penguinrandomhouse.com | rhcbooks.com

Library of Congress Cataloging-in-Publication Data is available upon request.
ISBN 979-8-217-03333-1 (hardcover) — ISBN 979-8-217-03334-8 (lib. bdg.) — ISBN 979-8-217-03335-5 (ebook)

The text of this book is set in 13.25-point ABC Arizona Mix.
The illustrations were rendered with watercolor, ink, crayon, cut paper, and a digital zhuzh.

Manufactured in China 10 9 8 7 6 5 4 3 2 1

The authorized representative in the EU for product safety and compliance is Penguin Random House Ireland, Morrison Chambers, 32 Nassau Street, Dublin D02 YH68, Ireland, https://eu-contact.penguin.ie.

Random House Children's Books supports the First Amendment and celebrates the right to read.

Hello there!
I'm Sharon McMahon. It's said like McWoman, except it's McMan. I'm happy you're here, because you're about to meet so many interesting people in this book—not the presidents but ordinary people. Some of them were courageous teenagers, some were teachers (like me!), some were incredible athletes, and some were amazing writers. All of them were important, just like you are, in ways both small and mighty.
Welcome, and let's dive in!

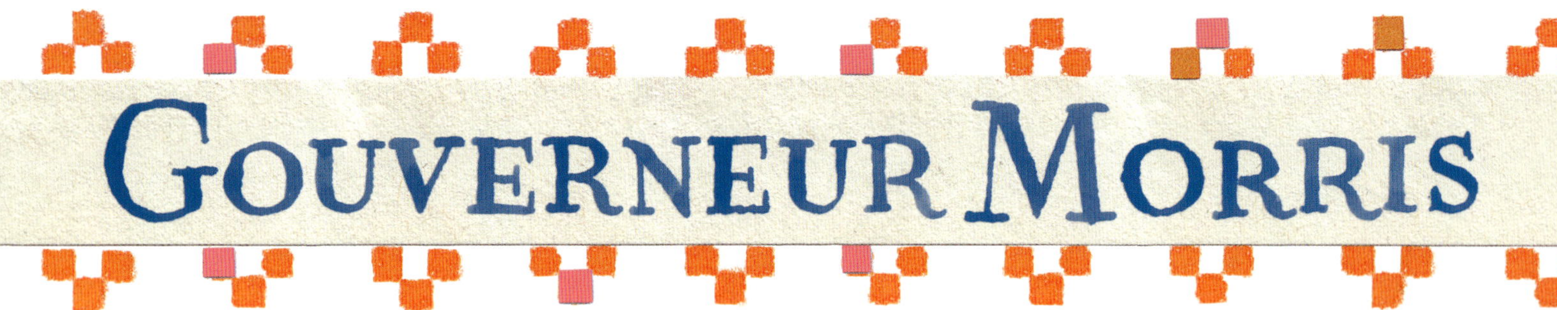

Gouverneur Morris

Gouverneur Morris yelled. His horses spooked and ran away without even realizing that Gouverneur's leg was tangled in their reins.

When he woke up, Gouverneur discovered that his lower leg had been replaced by a wooden one. But he didn't let this stop him from dancing the night away with his many friends, or from using his talents as a writer.

Later, when the United States needed to write a constitution, leaders asked each other who they could call for help in writing such an important document. "Gouverneur Morris," they all said.

Gouverneur used a quill to write something that changed the course of history. He scratched "We the people"—words that meant something extraordinary. Power would be in their hands alone, and the United States would never again be ruled by a terrible king.

We the People

Ida Lewis

I don't like the looks of that, Ida Lewis thought. From inside the lighthouse, she saw a sailboat in danger of capsizing in the cold waters of the Atlantic. Her instincts were right: Soon the four teenage boys had fallen into the rocky ocean, the waves washing over their heads.

Ida was only fifteen. She may have been small, but she was mighty. She sprang into action, leaping from the rocks near the lighthouse and into the rowboat her family kept tied nearby.

She pulled on the oars as hard as she could until the tops of the boys' heads were near enough to touch. They spluttered and gasped, panicking that they might never get back to shore.

Ida reached into the water and, with a strength she didn't even know she had, seized each of the boys by the shirt and hauled them into her rowboat.

As a lighthouse keeper and perhaps the best swimmer in Rhode Island, Ida rescued dozens of people who needed help. She saved so many lives that, one day, President Ulysses S. Grant rowed his own boat out to see her, tipping his hat to the lady called the

VIRGINIA RANDOLPH

The superintendent pointed to the tiny building and said, “Mountain Road School.”

Virginia stared. The building looked like no one had loved it for a very long time. It had a driveway covered with thick mud, and Virginia’s feet sank down until her shoes were covered. She yanked each foot out with a giant *schloooooop.*

“Just do the next needed thing,” Virginia whispered to herself. So she drove her buggy into town, hoisted the heavy bags of gravel all by herself, and then spread the stones smoothly with a rake. She introduced herself to all the parents so they would know there was a teacher who cared. “The children like coming to school,” Virginia told anyone who would listen.

Virginia kept doing the next needed thing, like helping children learn their letter sounds and how to read books full of adventure stories. She taught them to bake bread and sew quilts. By the time Virginia was an old woman, she'd had so many students that the sad little school building had been replaced by a large one made of bricks.

And the superintendent made sure the school was renamed

THE
VIRGINIA RANDOLPH
TRAINING ACADEMY

in honor of the woman who always did what she could for as many people as she could. The school is still there today.

Katharine Lee Bates

"KAAAAAAATIEEEEEE!" she heard her mother yell. Katie was hiding again, this time under the lilac bushes down the street from her house.

she heard her brother calling. But Katie didn't want to help her mother with the mending and the cooking. She wanted to write and to learn and to ask questions. Katie wanted to "study and study and study and know and know and know."

When Katie got older, she had a chance that many girls before her had never had: She went to high school and then college. She became a professor and traveled all over the world, feeling the slosh of waves against a ship or the *clack clack clack* of a train beneath her.

On one trip, she saw the most glorious scenery outside the train window. Cities blurred past, and so did mountains, farms, and lakes. An idea came to her. She took everything she had learned about the majesty of America and wrote a poem. People loved it so much, they set it to music and made it into a song.

It goes:

O beautiful for spacious skies,
For amber waves of grain . . .

Katie used her talent—not for sewing but for words—and she did something that helped millions of people see the beauty of the home they shared.

Ida B. Wells-Barnett

Ida Wells's friends told her, "If you get married and have babies, you won't be able to do your important work."

Ida B. Wells had a very important career. Not only was she a newspaper reporter who wrote about injustice, but she was also a suffragist, trying to help women of all races gain the right to vote. People loved to hear her speak, and she was excellent at it, traveling the country by train, marching in parades, giving interviews, and going to meetings with the president.

She didn't listen to her friends. She got married, hyphenating her last name to Wells-Barnett, and had children anyway.

She brought her baby on her trips, holding him and feeding him as the train chugged along. When it stopped at a station, the bustle of the city filled her ears. She looked around for the nurse she had arranged to care for her baby while she spoke, waving when she spotted her. "This is Charles," she said, introducing her charming baby. "Thank you for helping me with him."

"Ladies and gentlemen," Ida began, glancing around. The people in the crowd shushed each other to be quiet, listening attentively. Ida's audiences didn't want to miss a word of what she had to say.

MARÍA DE LÓPEZ

María shouted in Spanish. *WHY?*

All her life, María had been asking por qué? Why is the sun in the sky? Why can't I travel anywhere I wish? Why shouldn't women be allowed to vote?

When fighting started far across the ocean, María wanted to help. The army told her no. Again, she asked the same question: Why? Why can't I drive an ambulance to help soldiers in France who are hurt?

Eventually, the Red Cross, a group that helps people during wars and emergencies, taught women to fix ambulances when they broke down. Soon, women like María were dodging potholes, dropping patients off at the hospital, where doctors and nurses waited to help. She was scared, but she was brave.

When people back home heard that María had sailed across the ocean and rescued soldiers from a burning building, they put her face on the front of the newspaper. And when María boarded a ship home after the fighting stopped, she held a special medal of commendation that she had earned for her bravery. Everyone who saw it knew that sometimes the bravest thing you can do is ask "Why?"

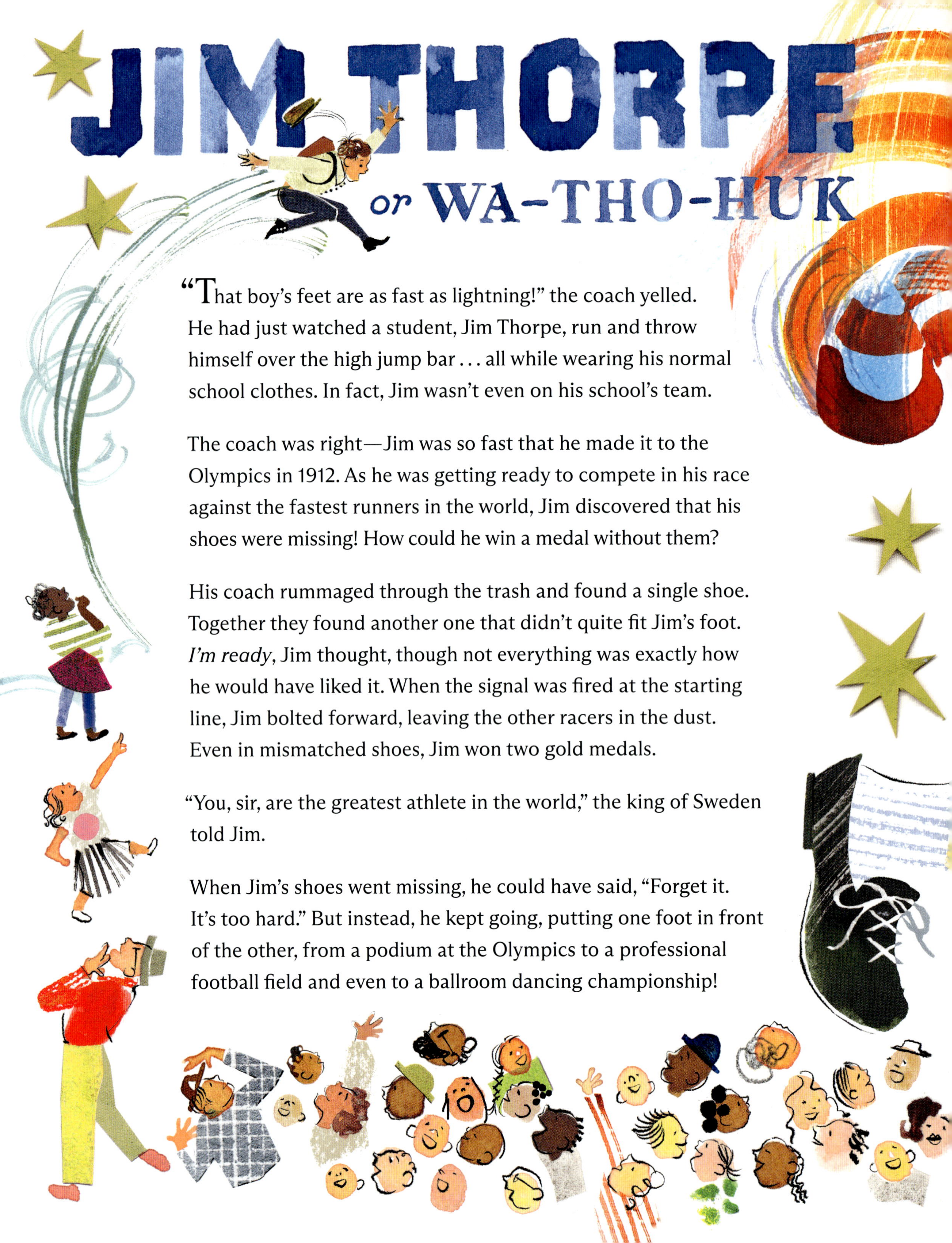

JIM THORPE or WA-THO-HUK

"That boy's feet are as fast as lightning!" the coach yelled. He had just watched a student, Jim Thorpe, run and throw himself over the high jump bar . . . all while wearing his normal school clothes. In fact, Jim wasn't even on his school's team.

The coach was right—Jim was so fast that he made it to the Olympics in 1912. As he was getting ready to compete in his race against the fastest runners in the world, Jim discovered that his shoes were missing! How could he win a medal without them?

His coach rummaged through the trash and found a single shoe. Together they found another one that didn't quite fit Jim's foot. *I'm ready*, Jim thought, though not everything was exactly how he would have liked it. When the signal was fired at the starting line, Jim bolted forward, leaving the other racers in the dust. Even in mismatched shoes, Jim won two gold medals.

"You, sir, are the greatest athlete in the world," the king of Sweden told Jim.

When Jim's shoes went missing, he could have said, "Forget it. It's too hard." But instead, he kept going, putting one foot in front of the other, from a podium at the Olympics to a professional football field and even to a ballroom dancing championship!

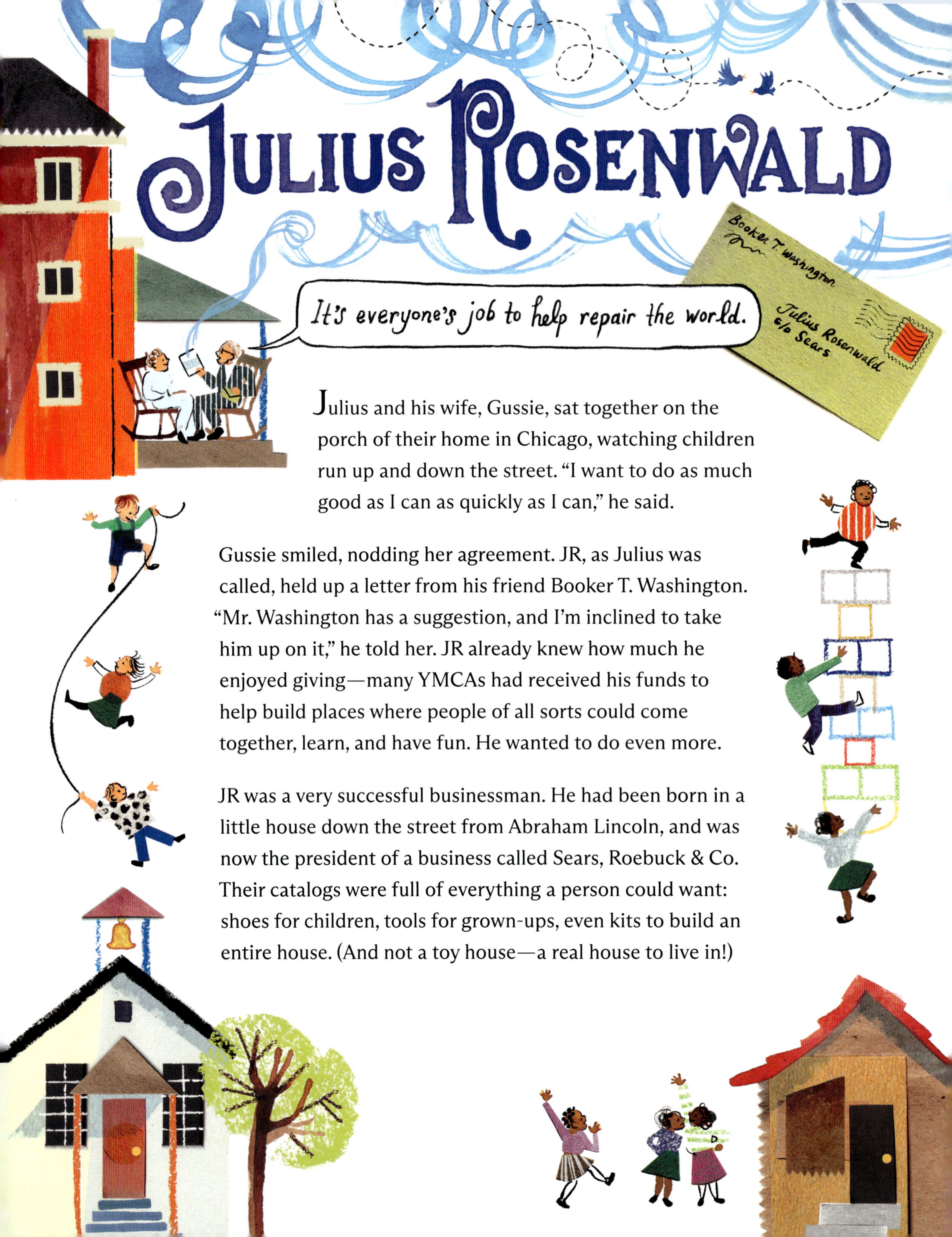

Julius Rosenwald

Julius and his wife, Gussie, sat together on the porch of their home in Chicago, watching children run up and down the street. "I want to do as much good as I can as quickly as I can," he said.

Gussie smiled, nodding her agreement. JR, as Julius was called, held up a letter from his friend Booker T. Washington. "Mr. Washington has a suggestion, and I'm inclined to take him up on it," he told her. JR already knew how much he enjoyed giving—many YMCAs had received his funds to help build places where people of all sorts could come together, learn, and have fun. He wanted to do even more.

JR was a very successful businessman. He had been born in a little house down the street from Abraham Lincoln, and was now the president of a business called Sears, Roebuck & Co. Their catalogs were full of everything a person could want: shoes for children, tools for grown-ups, even kits to build an entire house. (And not a toy house—a real house to live in!)

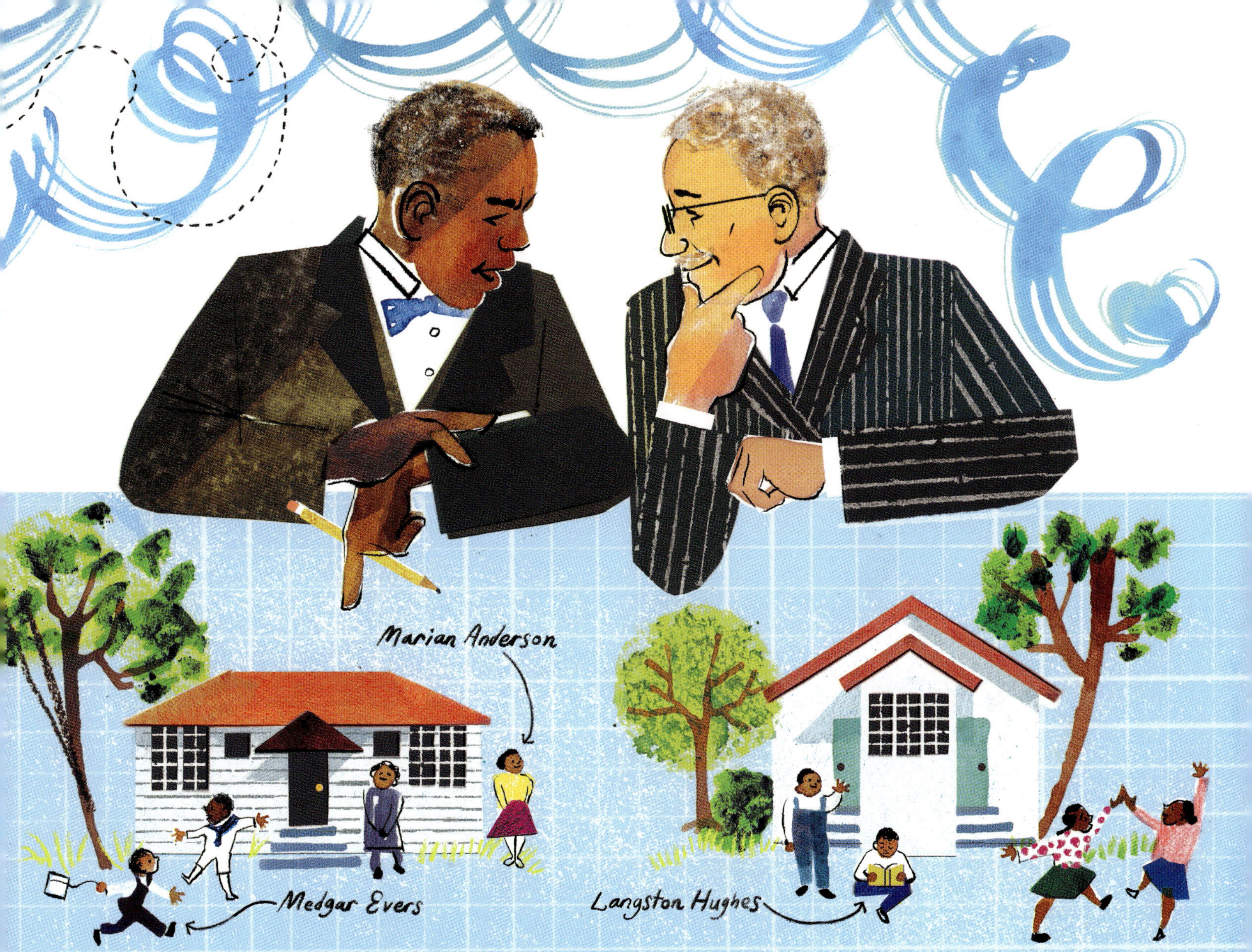
Marian Anderson
Medgar Evers
Langston Hughes

He wrote back to Booker T. Washington, and they came up with a plan to build five thousand schools across the American South, in places where Black children had not been able to get an education before. In each city that needed a school, residents took the plans from JR and Booker and helped to build a place where children could study and grow.

Maya Angelou
John Lewis

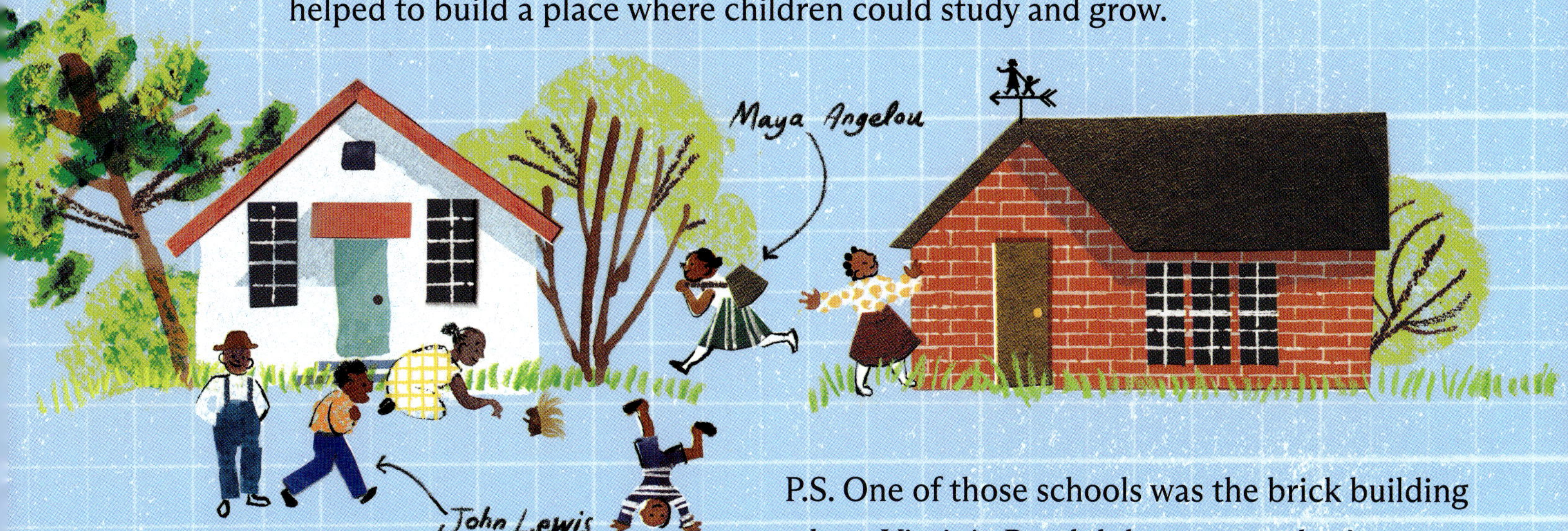

P.S. One of those schools was the brick building where Virginia Randolph was a teacher!

NORMAN MINETA

the scoutmaster yelled. Norm and his friend Alan were laughing so loudly that they woke up all the boys in their tents. They were at Heart Mountain, a camp in Wyoming where Norm and his family had been forced to live.

They had been called an enemy because they were Japanese Americans during a time when the United States was fighting against Japan. The Minetas, and more than 100,000 people like them, were made to leave their homes, businesses, and schools until the conflict ended.

Alan's family lived near Heart Mountain, and when he heard that his scout troop would be visiting the camp, he was scared. Until he met Norm.

When they grew up, Alan wrote Norm a letter, congratulating him on being elected mayor of San Jose, California. And not long after, Alan and Norm took their friendship somewhere else: to Washington, DC, where they walked through the marble halls of Congress, laughing together. Alan and Norm didn't always agree, but they always respected each other.

More than forty years after Japanese Americans were finally released from the unjust camps, Norm, Alan, and other members of Congress passed a bill to help make up for the wrongs done to Japanese Americans during the war. Alan knew that if America were to be just, he would have to work for justice for people who weren't like him.

When Norm and Alan got to be old men, retired from their jobs, they still had fun together. "We see each other and we just begin to laugh," Norm said.

Septima Clark

ANNA

“And what letter is this?” Septima asked her student, who was a grandmother.

A. And that is an N and another N and an A. It spells Anna. That’s my name.

Septima’s heart had never felt so proud. She lived in a place where many Black adults did not have the opportunity to learn to read as children, and now Septima was teaching them.

She made up a special way to help so that no one felt silly or embarrassed for not knowing their letters. The adults knew they could trust Septima with the secret they had tried to hide.

When they were done with their lessons with Miss Septima, not only could they read and write, they could vote and run for office, and teach others to do the same.

Septima didn’t only teach grown-ups to read; she also taught them how to organize for civil rights so all Americans could be treated equally, as they are meant to be. She taught them how to work with people who didn’t agree with them, because she knew that people could learn a different way.

A B C D E F G H I J K L M N

I have learned that I can work with my enemies,
not just tolerate them, because they might
have a change of heart at any moment.
OPQRSTU WXYZ

Roberto Clemente

Roberto Clemente counted.

“What are you doing?” his baseball teammate asked.

“Sorting my fan mail,” Roberto answered. Roberto Clemente was one of the greatest baseball players of all time. When he was growing up in Puerto Rico, his family was very poor, and his mother often had to get up at one o’clock in the morning to get to work. But she taught her son that it was his job to leave the world a better place than he found it.

So when Roberto got fan mail, he sorted it into piles. Into one, he put the letters from children, which he tried his best to answer.

And then he went through all the children's letters to see if any of them were sick and in the hospital. He wanted to be sure to visit them when his team traveled to their city so he could help them feel better by lifting their spirits.

Roberto hoped that someday the children would get well and do what they could to brighten the day of someone else who needed it. Playing baseball was about so much more than hitting a ball with a bat: It was about community, confidence, and camaraderie.

CLAUDETTE COLVIN

"Claudette! Here!" her friend said, pointing to a seat on the city bus. School let out early that day, and Claudette was thrilled to be in the sunshine and not inside a classroom. She weaved her way down the aisle of the bus, dodging backpacks and stepping over books, taking a seat near her friend.

In 1955, some people believed the wrong thing: They thought that Black people and white people were not equal. And when a white woman got on the bus and demanded that Claudette give up the seat she paid for, Claudette wouldn't do it. She knew what the woman was asking wasn't fair.

The police came and dragged Claudette off the bus. Claudette worried about what could happen to her, but when she was brought before a judge, she held her head high and told the truth.

The rules of the bus were unfair, and she knew it. The judge listened to Claudette's testimony, his brow furrowed.
Her courage to testify in a courtroom soon led to
something much bigger than one bus:
It led to the rules being changed so
they were fair for *everyone*.

Someday, you will need to have courage to do the next needed thing, whether that's helping a friend at school, speaking up for what's right, even if it feels scary, or making the right choice, even when it's hard. And when that day arrives, tomorrow or many years from now, I hope you'll think back to the people you met on these pages and be reminded that you, too, can be mighty, no matter how big or how small you are.

Timeline

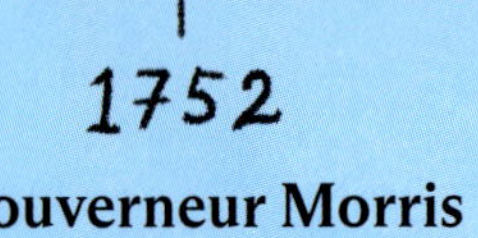

1752
Gouverneur Morris is born.

1780
Gouverneur Morris is injured in a carriage accident.

1787
Gouverneur Morris serves at the Constitutional Convention.

1862
Ida B. Wells is born. (July)
Julius Rosenwald is born. (August)

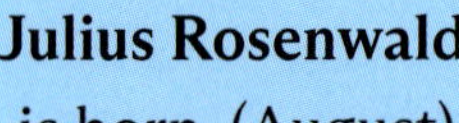

1869
President Grant visits **Ida Lewis**'s lighthouse.

1870
Virginia Randolph is born.

1881
María de López is born.

1897
Ida B. Wells travels by train with her baby.

1898
Septima Clark is born.

1912
Jim Thorpe loses his shoes at the Olympics. (July)
Julius Rosenwald partners with Booker T. Washington to build schools. (September)

1939
Claudette Colvin is born.

1942
Norman Mineta meets Alan Simpson.

1955
Claudette Colvin refuses to give up her seat on the bus. (March)
Roberto Clemente begins playing Major League Baseball. (April)

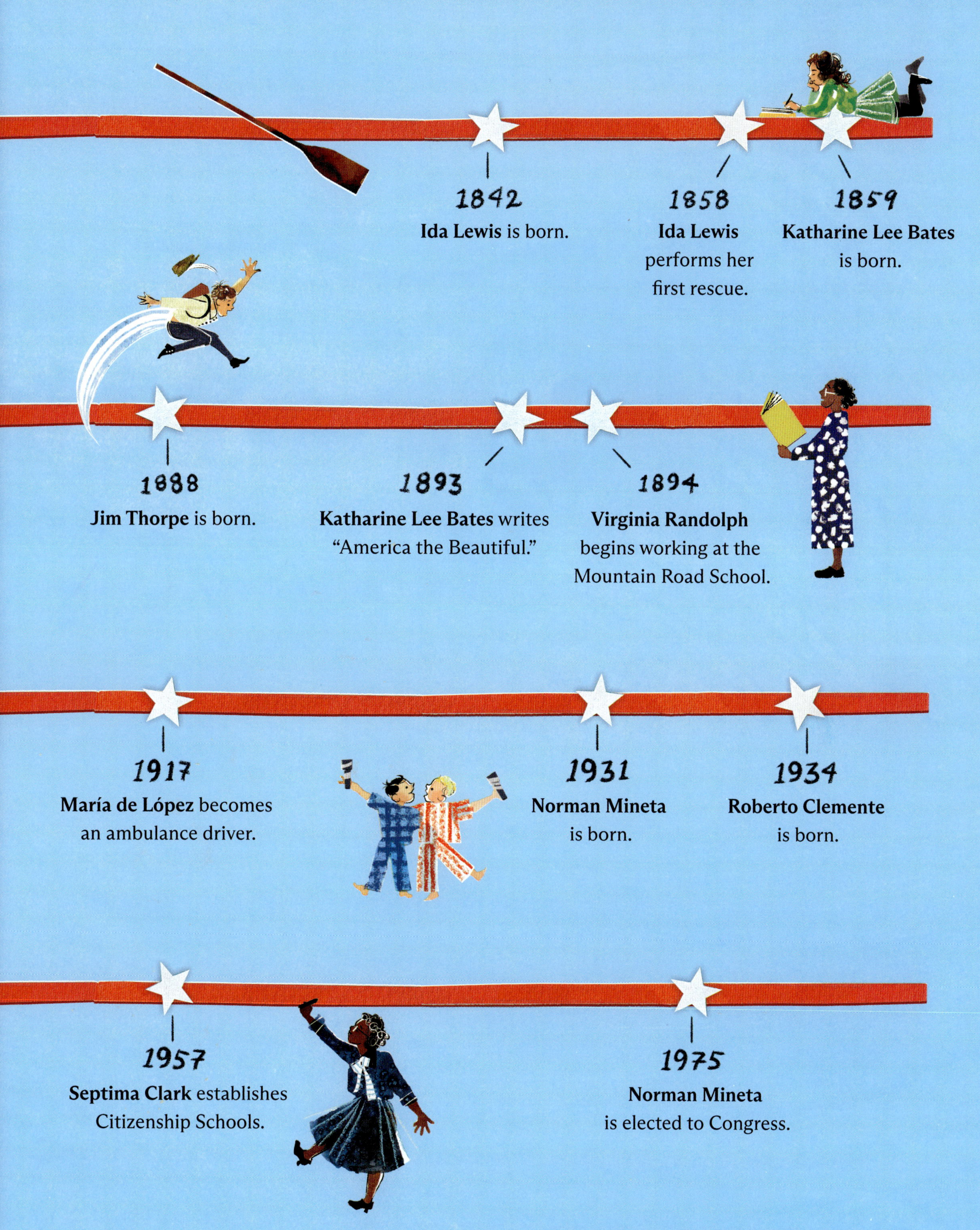

1842
Ida Lewis is born.

1858
Ida Lewis performs her first rescue.

1859
Katharine Lee Bates is born.

1888
Jim Thorpe is born.

1893
Katharine Lee Bates writes "America the Beautiful."

1894
Virginia Randolph begins working at the Mountain Road School.

1917
María de López becomes an ambulance driver.

1931
Norman Mineta is born.

1934
Roberto Clemente is born.

1957
Septima Clark establishes Citizenship Schools.

1975
Norman Mineta is elected to Congress.

Selected Bibliography

"The Annenberg Guide to the United States Constitution: What It Says, What It Means." Annenberg Classroom. Accessed August 2025. annenbergclassroom.org/constitution/.

Brandman, Mariana. "Maria Guadalupe Evangelina de Lopez." National Women's History Museum, 2020. womenshistory.org/education-resources/biographies/maria-guadalupe-evangelina-de-lopez.

Charron, Katherine Mellen. *Freedom's Teacher: The Life of Septima Clark.* University of North Carolina Press, 2012.

Feiler, Andrew. *A Better Life for Their Children: Julius Rosenwald, Booker T. Washington, and the 4,978 Schools That Changed America.* University of Georgia Press, 2021.

Giddings, Paula J. *Ida: A Sword Among Lions: Ida B. Wells and the Campaign Against Lynching.* Amistad, 2009.

Hoose, Phillip. *Claudette Colvin: Twice Toward Justice.* Square Fish, 2010.

Maraniss, David. *Clemente: The Passion and Grace of Baseball's Last Hero.* Simon & Schuster Paperbacks, 2007.

Maraniss, David. *Path Lit by Lightning: The Life of Jim Thorpe.* Simon & Schuster, 2023.

Ponder, Melinda M. *Katharine Lee Bates: From Sea to Shining Sea.* Windy City, 2017.

Skomal, Lenore. *The Lighthouse Keeper's Daughter: The Remarkable True Story of American Heroine Ida Lewis.* Globe Pequot, 2010.

"Virginia Estelle Randolph." Virginia Humanities. September 8, 2021. virginiahumanities.org/2021/09/virginia-estelle-randolph/.

Warren, Andrea. *Enemy Child: The Story of Norman Mineta, a Boy Imprisoned in a Japanese American Internment Camp During World War II.* Margaret Ferguson Books/Holiday House, 2021.

Source Notes for Quotations

The quotes below are pulled directly from the sources listed. The rest are invented dialogue based on in-depth research.

"Just do the next needed thing"
Daniel Kreisman, "The Next Needed Thing: The Impact of the Jeanes Fund on Black Schooling in the South, 1900–1930," *The Journal of Human Resources* 52, no. 2 (2017): 573–620, jstor.org/stable/26450455.

"... study and study and study and know and know and know."
Dorothy Burgess, *Dream and Deed: The Story of Katharine Lee Bates* (University of Oklahoma Press: 1952), 32.

"¿Por qué?"
Political Equality League, "Dese a la mujer de California el derecho de votar," Women's Suffrage and Equal Rights Collection (Claremont, 1911).

"You, sir, are the greatest athlete in the world."
"Sport: The Greatest Athlete," *TIME*, April 6, 1953, time.com/archive/6620473/sport-the-greatest-athlete/.

"We see each other and we just begin to laugh."
"A Friendship Born in One of America's Darkest Hours," *CBS Sunday Morning*, December 9, 2018, cbsnews.com/news/alan-simpson-norman-mineta-friendship-born-out-of-japanese-american-internment-camp/.